W … SO
S … ECIAL…?

DAVID DAY

LION EDUCATIONAL
Oxford · Batavia · Sydney

Published by
Lion Publishing plc
Sandy Lane West, Oxford, England
ISBN 0 7459 1365 2
Albatross Books Pty Ltd
PO Box 320, Sutherland, NSW 2232, Australia
ISBN 0 7324 0047 3

First edition 1989
Reprinted 1990

Quotations and references
Pages 14–15: the author has used the following sources in preparing this material: E. Cashmore, *Rastaman*, published by Allen and Unwin, 1979; D. Guiton, 'Seeing Ras Tafari plain: a phenomenological viewpoint', in *British Journal of Educational Studies*, Vol. 33, No.3, pp.262–77, October 1985.
The quotations on pages 18–19 are from: A. Pacheco and A. Francione, 'The silver spring monkeys', in P. Singer (ed), *In Defence of Animals*, p.139, published by Basil Blackwell, 1985; and H. Spira, 'Fighting to win', in Singer, *op. cit.*, p.194.
The quotations on pages 24 and 25 are from the following sources: [1]Isaiah 6:1–5; [2]Mark 16:8; [3]M. Rodinson, *Mohammed*, p.71, Penguin Books, 1961; [4]J. Bowker, *Worlds of Faith*, p. 117, BBC Ariel Books, 1983; [5]J. Bowker, p.113; [6]D. Hay, *Exploring Inner Space*, p.133, Penguin Books, 1982; [7]E. Robinson (ed), *Living the Questions*, p.76, RERU, Oxford, 1978; [8]E. Robinson, p.107.

Illustrations
Simon Jenkins pp. 5, 8, 11, 17, 18, 25;
Kim Raymond pp. 6, 29;
all others Tony Cantale Graphics

Photographs
Caroline Austin p. 9; Barnaby's Picture Library pp. 22, 23 (bottom), /Hubertus Kanus p. 23 (top), /Brian Gibbs p. 26; BBC Hulton Picture Library pp. 4, 10, 16; *Catholic Herald* p. 23 (centre); DAS Photo/David Simpson cover, pp. 30, 31; Greenpeace/Gleizes p. 19; Lynx p. 20; Network Photographers/Katalin Arkell p. 15; David Townsend Photography p. 3

Printed in Yugoslavia

Contents

SECTION 1

SECTION 2

SECTION 3

Teenage tears after break-in

DISTRAUGHT

Yesterday afternoon, while she was at school, thieves raided the bedroom of Miss Tracy Blenkinsop, the fun-loving, 15-year-old daughter of Mr and Mrs Albert Blenkinsop of 96, Railway Terrace, Blackton, and made off with a number of items. A distraught and tearful Tracy told our reporter:

★★★★★★★★★★★★★★★

'I'm absolutely distraught and tearful. They took everything valuable that I possess. I can't think why. I'm just a fun-loving 15-year-old. It's not as if they'd get anything much for the things they took. They just had sentimental value.'

★★★★★★★★★★★★★★★

Among the items stolen were:

A bus ticket
a signed photograph
a finger nail
a postcard (postmarked 'Isle of Man')
a sea shell
a coca cola can (empty)
a shoelace (white) with three knots tied in it

POLICE BAFFLED

Local police confessed they were baffled. 'This kind of break-in just doesn't seem to have a motive,' admitted Detective Constable Pringle of the Blackton Constabulary.

Little things mean a lot

We'll leave Tracy weeping all over the reporter for a bit. You probably weren't very impressed by what was stolen, anyway.

But we can understand why she was upset. We all have bits and pieces which we wouldn't like to lose, because, one way or another, they matter to us. They're important. They've got 'sentimental value'. We take them seriously and we expect other people to do so as well. We don't take kindly to having them laughed at or messed about.

Believe it or not, some people actually went more than thirty times to see *The Sound of Music*. Not your cup of tea? Maybe it's the Rovers, or rock music that's special for you . . .

▶Stephen has a collection of records. Not just any records. He has every single disk that's ever been cut by Sid Flem and the Catarrhs. The collection is priceless – to Stephen. (His mates can't stand Sid Flem.)

▶Andrea is about to go to Art College. All her belongings are stuffed into her Dad's car. Her posters, records, love letters, keepsakes, clothes, back numbers of *Wow!* magazine, fifteen old Mills and Boons, thirty-eight different pairs of shoes, fourteen tee shirts, two old macs (a snip at 30p from the Oxfam shop) and an assortment of designer jeans. But most important of all, top of the heap, comes Pilby. He's a large, moth-eaten Teddy Bear with one ear.

Sometimes these special things are bigger than objects. They're **Places.**

▶There isn't a Liverpool supporter in the world who doesn't thrill at the sound of Anfield. Someone else will react to Goodison Park or White Hart Lane or Old Trafford or Carrow Road or Roker Park or Hillsborough or Alderman Hooggie Municipal Park, home of Drain Street Rovers.

▶The places don't have to be famous. Four small children have a den down on the Nature Reserve. No one knows about it. It's theirs. It's special. One day they'll grow out of playing wild men of the woods but they'll still remember the den as a special place.

▶There's a tree in Loughall Wood that's special to Fiona. It was on this very spot that the gorgeous Nigel (oh joy) took her tenderly in his arms and asked in his sexy voice if he could borrow her Physics notes. 'Shall we go on doing this?' he breathed. 'You doing the work and me copying up afterwards?' 'Oh yes, oh yes,' she moaned.

People are special as well.

▶One boy wrote: 'My Mum and Dad are the most important people in the world to me, even though they get up my nose sometimes – as I do theirs.'

▶A girl said: 'I've got posters of Nick Shaw all over my bedroom. Ooh he's lovely. I'd love to meet him, though I'm sure I wouldn't know what to say if I did.'

▶Meanwhile in another bedroom, Moggo, superstar of the future, has plastered his walls with pictures of Frank Bruno and Daley Thompson.

▶While down in the bike sheds Baz continues to spray 'Ange 4 me – she's the gratist' to the despair of the caretaker and his English teacher.

It's only a little jump from these to the **Ideas** or **Principles** which matter to us. These are the things we get steamed up about.

▶It might be 'pupil power' or 'a woman's right to choose' or 'Clouseau fans against the beumb'.

▶'It's a matter of principle' we say, as we protest or march or write letters or knock on doors or just argue with other people. These ideas are important; they *matter* to us.

And then there are **hobbies, activities** and **interests** which dominate our lives: dancing, martial arts, fishing, collecting beer mats, train spotting, dismantling motor bikes, ice skating, playing the flute or the guitar, weight training, cookery.

FOLLOW UP

1 Turn back to the list of items that were taken from Tracy's bedroom. Your job is to explain why each of the objects is special to Tracy. Work out your reasons in pairs. When you're ready one of you will have to *be* Tracy and explain to the rest of the group why you feel the way you do. Put in as much detail as you can; try to link up as many objects as possible into a connected story. Be imaginative. If the bus ticket was given you by the driver of a Martian space ship, well, OK then. (But it sounds as if you've been watching too much telly.)

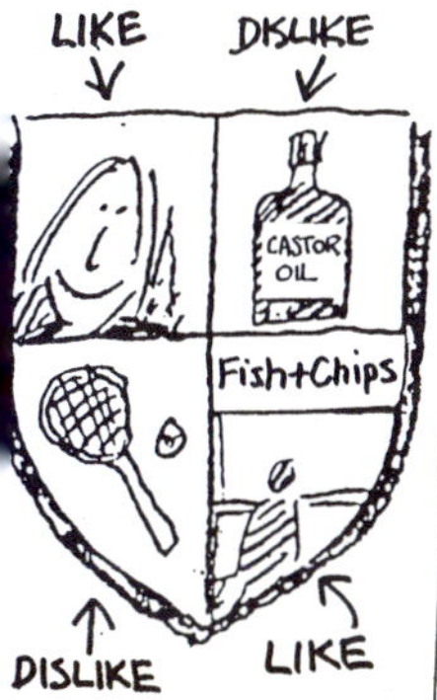

2 Produce a map of what is special to you. This can take a number of forms:

▶You can design a shield which contains drawings in the different quarters of what you like and dislike, what you value, what you are good at. It will need a motto summing up the sort of person you are.

▶Or you could produce a montage of cuttings from magazines which express different sides of your personality. Here you might use colours and shapes as well as actual pictures to make your point.

▶Or draw up a 'personal forcefield'. In the middle of a piece of paper put a cross. This represents the very centre of your personality. Now put in the names of four people, four objects, four beliefs, four activities and four places at different distances from the centre. The more important they are to you, the nearer to the centre you should put them. Try to get a range of items. Some very near, some mid-distance, and the things you don't care much about round the outside.

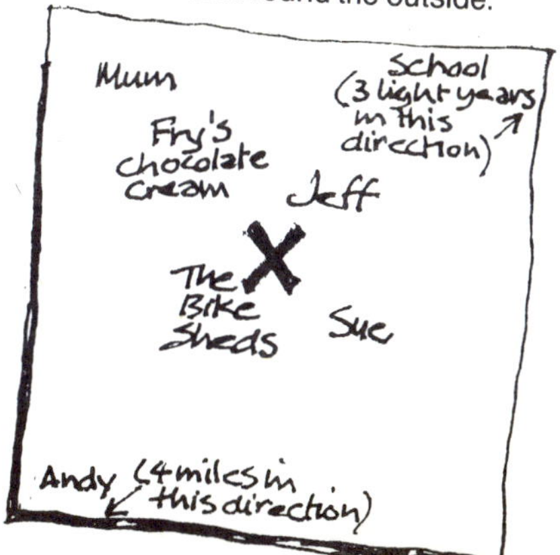

▶Now take your partner's list and draw up *his* or *her* 'forcefield'. Did you get it right? How well do you know your friend?

Expressing your values

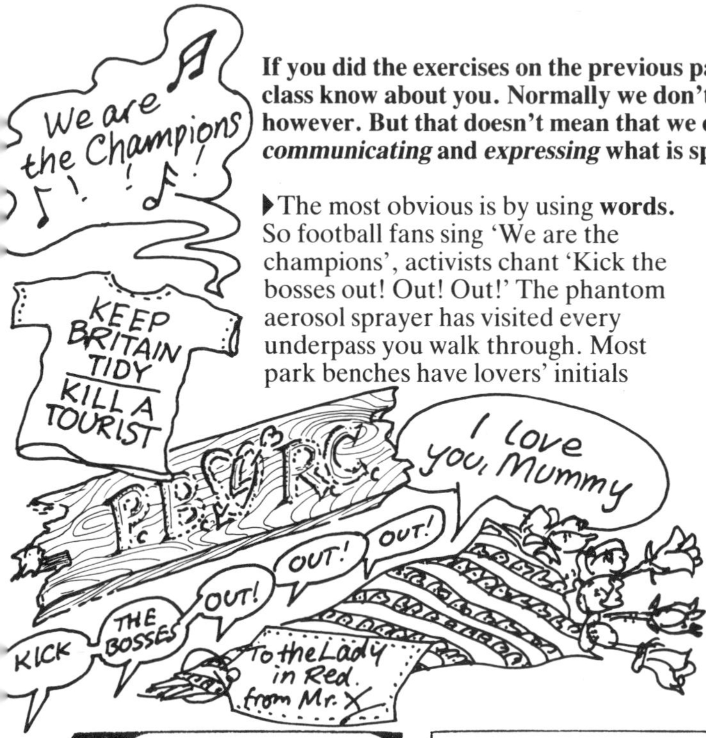

If you did the exercises on the previous page then by now a lot of people in the class know about you. Normally we don't do anything as formal as an exercise however. But that doesn't mean that we don't have dozens of ways of *communicating* and *expressing* what is special and important to us.

▶The most obvious is by using **words.** So football fans sing 'We are the champions', activists chant 'Kick the bosses out! Out! Out!' The phantom aerosol sprayer has visited every underpass you walk through. Most park benches have lovers' initials carved into them. The little boy says, 'I love you, Mummy'. Someone else says, 'I believe in saying what I think.' And tee shirts carry messages for all the world to read: 'Don't ASK', 'Make love not war'; 'Keep Britain tidy. Kill a tourist'; 'The only safe fast-breeder is a rabbit'.

▶But **actions** also give out messages. Protesters outside the Russian Embassy stand silently, holding lighted candles. Their actions tell the officials that they think it's important to release dissidents from Soviet prisons.

▶A good clue is what we spend our **money** on. A man buys an expensive

bottle of wine in order to celebrate an anniversary with his wife. Brown ale or tea from a tea bag won't do the job properly.

▶Another key factor is the amount of **time** we spend on what we say is important to us. You would expect someone who says she's fanatical about canoeing to spend most of her weekends actually on the water. A man says, 'I'm training for the London marathon', but every time you see him he's in the 'Queen's Legs' drinking pints. 'What's your weekly mileage?', you ask. 'Well, I walk the half mile to work on Tuesdays.' Hmmm . . . is success in the marathon *really* important to him?

▶Another clue is the **effort** that we put in. Scott is hoping to go off on a fishing trip with some of his mates. It's going to cost an arm and a leg. So he takes a job delivering newspapers. This means that he has to get up in the pitch dark all through the winter and trudge round in the ice, snow, fog, rain and hail. It's a deadly job and not specially well paid. But all this effort shows dramatically how much he cares about fishing.

▶Sometimes extra strong **reactions** will give the game away. It's not difficult to read between the lines of this dialogue:

▶ 'What d'ya think of the new girl, then?'
'Who? Sandra Thingy? She's OK, I s'pose.'
▶ 'Go on, she's fantastic!'
'I don't reckon her that much.'
▶ 'You couldn't take your eyes off her in double maths.'
'Who, me? Don't be daft. I hardly noticed her.'
▶ 'What you blushing for then?'
'Oh shut yer face.'
▶ 'Hey . . . you fancy her something rotten, don't you? You've gone all red.'
'I DON'T! I HAVEN'T! Will you shut up about her!'

FOLLOW UP

1 Draw a grid with five columns at the top across the page and five spaces down the page. At the top of each column put the headings: WORDS, ACTIONS, MONEY, TIME, EFFORT. In the left-hand margin put five activities or people that you think are special to you. You might put 'Fruit machines'; 'Gymnastics'; 'Horses'; 'Religion'; 'Linda'; 'Nick'; 'Making clothes' – anything could go in there. Now fill in the boxes for each item. What sort of things do you say about it? What do you do that shows it's special? How much money did it cost you last week? How much time did you spend on it last week? What sort of effort did you have to put in?

When you've completed the chart, get a friend to put your five special things into an order 1–5, working *only on the evidence of the chart*. Are there any surprises? Do Linda or Nick really mean less to you than fruit machines?

You might then discuss whether this way of working out what is really special to you is a sensible one. What would you say to someone who says, 'I don't care what the chart shows. X *is* important to me. It's just that I don't talk about it much, or spend any time or money or effort on it, or *do* very much about it.'?

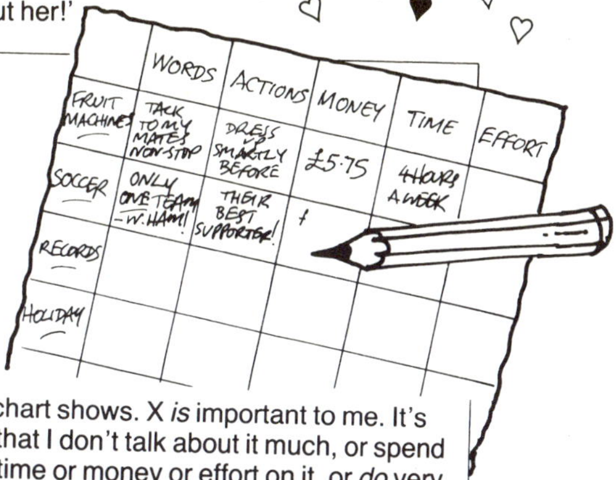

2 The clothes we wear express what we think is important. They give off *messages* and most people become experts at reading what people are *saying* through what they're *wearing*.

Give examples (a sketch with labels would be better) of what people would wear if they wanted to communicate the following messages:

▶'I'm just the sort of sensible boy/girl that you ought to give this office job to.'
▶'I don't care what the neighbours think.'
▶'Don't tangle with me, buster.'
▶'I've come to this party to enjoy myself.'

Values under attack

We've seen some of the ways in which we express our values, the things we think are special to us. We also looked at the possibility that we might be fooling ourselves. But what happens when the pressure is on?

We might *say* we stand for this or that idea, or *say* we care about this or that person or object. But when something which we say is important to us comes under attack, or when we have to make a deliberate choice between it and something else, then we can see immediately whether we are really committed or just talking as if we were.

Sometimes the pressure arises naturally. You can't do two things at the same time, for example:

- Angela wants to go to the match on Saturday afternoon *and* grab the chance of a driving lesson with her brother. Her brother can only manage 3.45 on Saturday afternoon. What is more important? Her decision will tell us.

- Lee can't get his hair cut really short for his camping holiday *and* grow it for his girlfriend, who likes it long and unmanageable. The way he sorts the conflict out will tell us, him and the girlfriend, what his values are.

- Ally is a fearless supporter of Witherstone Rovers. He chants 'We're coming to get you' at the opposition. He *also* cares about his health and safety. When the Rovers supporters invade the visitors' end, Ally makes sure he stays where he is.

As the old saying goes: 'You can't have your cake and eat it.'

These sorts of value conflicts come up all the time.

- Mandy has set her heart on being a vet. She knows that she needs to work hard for her GCSEs. She says that she's serious about passing. A month before the exams she gets the chance of a job, seven nights a week, in a local pub. She'd like the money and the job pays well. What should she do?

- The headteacher at Furzehill Comprehensive is having a blitz on tidiness. He insists that three boys in the fifth year get their hair cut. He even offers them money for the hairdresser. The boys like their hair the way it is; it's part of their image. The head gets stroppy and makes noises about suspension and references for employers.

▶Miss Thornton is 35 and has looked after her invalid mother for years. Because of this she has never married. She loves her mother but finds her 'a terrible tie'. A widower at the office where she works proposes to her. She likes him and realizes it's more or less her last chance to get married. 'It's important to me to have a life of my own,' she thinks. 'But I could never put mother into a home. She's important to me as well.'

▶Denise has a reputation for being a good listener. She likes this and is prepared to give a lot of her time to her friends' problems. But one friend, Vicky, threatens to take her over. 'She goes on and on,' complains Denise, 'I get stuck with her for hours. She gets terribly jealous if I spend time with anyone else and when I tell her about it, she sort of goes to pieces.'

▶Gerry prides himself on being loyal to his mates. 'I never let them down,' he says. One evening one of his friends was set on by a gang of youths who'd been looking for him. Gerry ran away. Actually, that's not quite true. He stood at a safe distance and threw stones at the gang. 'Not quite Sylvester Stallone but the best I could manage,' he said.

When you are under pressure about something that matters to you, what do you do? The Greenham women chose protest, in the cause of peace.

FOLLOW UP

1 Collect some examples from newspapers and magazines of situations where people have had to choose between two values, *both of which* have been important to them. Stick these on a large piece of paper as a montage. Try to give them a striking title.

2 Imagine someone sitting in a chair. Your task is to make him move. You are not allowed to touch him or the chair in any way. Brainstorm with a partner on different methods you might try. See if you can get 5 different ones (pretty good) or even 10 (brilliant). They have to be different; e.g. offering him £5 is the same method (appealing to his greed) as offering him £50.

3 The argument of this section is that anything we think is important has a *cost* to it. Work out the cost in time, money, risk, etc. of the following projects. Remember that most costs are hidden – that is, they're not obvious. Try to present your results in a visual form.

▶Winning an Olympic gold medal.
▶Staying in bed all day.
▶Something that you would personally very, very much like to achieve.

4 Which would you rather do?

▶Walk down the high street in your underwear, or get mugged?
▶Make a lot of money but be bed-ridden all your life, or be fit and healthy with hardly any money at all?
▶Kiss a frog (which might turn into a prince or princess but you never know with fairy tales or frogs), or play safe and make sure your face doesn't get slimy?
▶Be St Francis of Assisi and help humanity, or be Alexander the Great and rule the world?

When you've made your choices, try to work out the hidden values which are in conflict in the above examples.

Taking it all too far

So far we've looked at things that are special to us, with a glance at the values which other people think are important. You might have found yourself saying, 'Well, that's stupid' or 'I don't agree with that at all!' That's not surprising, in fact, it might even be a good thing.

Would you feel these people were going 'too far', if you knew they were, a) at a football match, b) at a Conservative Party Conference, c) at a religious service? Give your reasons!

But quite often we don't just disagree. We feel that someone's commitment to a value has gone too far. We have words to describe this. We say they're 'fanatical' or 'cranky'. They've got an 'obsession' over something. Of course one person's fanatic is another's hero or martyr. We can easily forget that the word 'fan' is short for 'fanatic'.

Can you tell the difference?

In 1987 thousands of 'wannerbees' waited for hours and hours at Heathrow to catch a glimpse of Madonna. They were fans. Were they fanatics? They were nicknamed 'wannerbees' because they kept up a non-stop chant of 'We wannerbe Madonna.' Would they have been better off doing something useful, being kind to animals, pressing wildflowers or helping old ladies?

Here are some examples of commitments taken to extremes. Are these people fanatics? Or just people with very strong beliefs? Should we pity them? Or treat them as heroes?

▸ During the Iran-Iraq war suicide boats packed full of explosives were used. The troops deliberately drove the boats into larger ships. They did this, even though they knew that they would die the minute the boats exploded.

▸ A Liverpool supporter once had his baby christened with all thirteen names of the team of that season (eleven regular team members plus two substitutes). Somewhere in Liverpool there's a 25-year-old man going about with thirteen names, which very few people have heard of.

▸ IRA hunger strikers have chosen to protest by refusing to take food. They have persisted in their refusal even to the point of death.

▶Teenage lovers, Gary Smith and Wendy Barclay, made a suicide pact rather than be separated.

▶A Japanese soldier continued to fight World War II up to twenty years after it had ended.

▶Buddhist monks protested against the war in Vietnam by drenching themselves in petrol and setting themselves alight.

▶Mrs Fairly, aged 69, lives alone in her terraced house except for ninety-three cats. She can't bear to turn away strays, even though the house looks and smells like the Corporation tip.

▶Park Soon-jai, 48, nicknamed 'Benevolent Mother' by her followers, was the leader of a religious cult which preached that the world was about to come to an end. One morning the bodies of thirty-three members were found neatly stacked in a Korean factory. They had all been strangled or poisoned in a murder-suicide pact. None appeared to have resisted.

FOLLOW UP

1 Discuss these examples in pairs or fours. Which of them seem fanatical to you? Are there any that you can sympathize with, even if you wouldn't go that far yourself? Are some of these examples more praiseworthy than others? If you had to give an example of fanaticism, what would it be? How can you judge between examples? Is it all just a matter of taste?

2 Few of us will admit to being a fanatic. But we don't like to think of ourselves as having no views, or being easy to push around. Some things are so important we will resist enormous pressure in order to hold to them. Others don't matter to us much and we give them up easily. But there's usually a sliding-scale of pressure.

What cause, principle, idea, value, person, would you *like to think* you would be prepared to . . .

▶get told off by your teacher for?
▶be kept in for?
▶lose your friends for?
▶get sent to prison for?
▶die for?

Notice it says, 'would you like to think'. What we would *actually* do in real life is something entirely different. You might be a big softy *really* but you might still *like to think* you would be prepared to lose all your friends if they kept on saying rotten things about your Mum.

Why are special things special?

There's no end to the things, places, people or ideas which can be special or important to someone. But we might ask, 'Why are special things special? How can quite ordinary things become so important to us?'

Here's one way of explaining it. It's not the only way. See if it makes sense to you.

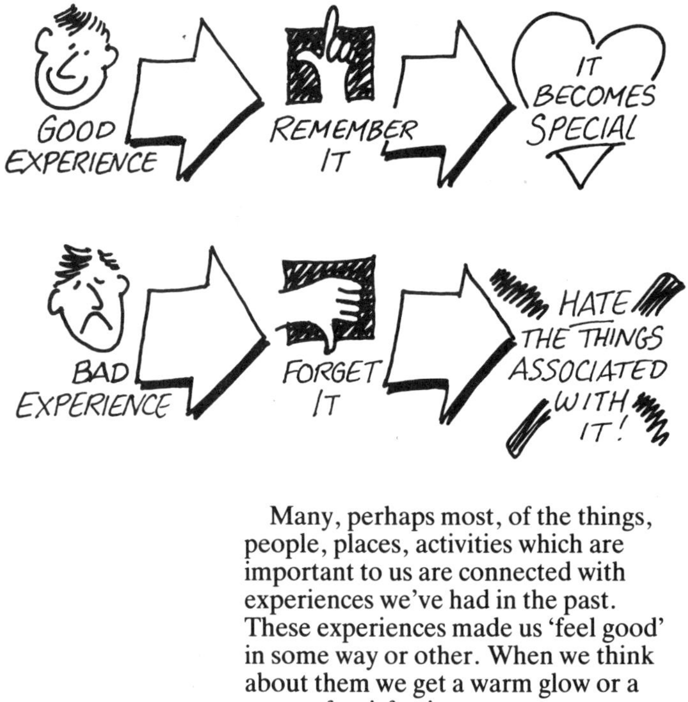

Many, perhaps most, of the things, people, places, activities which are important to us are connected with experiences we've had in the past. These experiences made us 'feel good' in some way or other. When we think about them we get a warm glow or a sense of satisfaction.

The 'feeling good' is not just to do with the past. If it seems that there's a fair chance that the good experience might be repeated, we try it again. We're more likely to give something pleasant a second go. Then, if we're rewarded enough times, we get into a habit. For example, Gerry likes fruit machines. he's won just often enough to make him go back again and again.

In the same way we're not likely to repeat 'bad experiences'. We'll avoid them as much as possible and not like to remember objects, places or people connected with them. For example, Dinah went to a disco and hated it. She didn't know anyone, isn't very good at dancing, and ended up spending the evening in the loo. As a result she avoids discos and claims that she 'can't stand the people who go there'.

Unfortunately, sometimes an experience is 'good' and 'bad' at the same time. We might like to risk the bad in order to get the good. Or half enjoy the good, even though the bad is offputting. Phil is now smoking about ten a day. It's expensive and he has to make sure his father doesn't catch him at it. So he feels guilty and doesn't enjoy having to be careful. But he also feels good about smoking. His friends all smoke and he feels fairly adult when he's got a fag in.

These examples suggest that we seek out and repeat 'good experiences' and avoid 'bad' ones.

But what makes you 'feel good' varies from person to person. One person's 'good' experience might be poison to someone else.

So what sort of things make you feel good?

"I feel good when I feel I belong. That is, when I feel safe and secure; when I can be myself and don't have to put on an act."

"I feel good when I feel I'm recognized as an individual. That is, when I'm not ignored. When people accept I've got ideas of my own, that I won't be pushed around, that I've got a character. I'm not just a shapeless blob."

"I feel good when I feel I am likeable. That is, when people praise me or show approval. When they show warmth, laugh at my jokes, take my opinions seriously. When I feel I'm OK."

"I feel good when I feel I am good at something. That is, when I succeed at something or show I am competent. When I'm good at an activity, reach a target or cope well with a challenge."

If these ideas are right then . . . Anything or anybody you think is important will be connected up to one of the 'feeling good' experiences. Something that seems totally insignificant to everyone else can be very important to you
- because it reminds you of a time when you felt good
- because it is a part of a package of things which make you feel good
- because it is the exact opposite of something which makes you feel bad.

Somehow there's going to be some sort of 'pay off'.

FOLLOW UP

1 Try to think of at least one example of a situation when

- you felt you belonged;
- somebody praised you;
- somebody showed warmth or friendliness towards you;
- you felt competent and handled a situation well;
- you took a risk and came through OK;
- you stood up for yourself and asserted yourself in some way.

And try to think of one example of a time when

- you felt out of things;
- you were humiliated;
- you were treated badly by an adult;
- you failed at something;
- you were made to feel you were no good.

What has been the result of these experiences? Some of them might not have affected you at all. But try to list all the results, as you see them, even if they seem unimportant. For example, a first former was shouted at by his Art Teacher on the very first day at his new school. As a result he hated Art, disliked the teacher — and was just that bit less confident in school.

2 Think of an object, a place, a person or an activity which is important to you. Try to show how it links up with your 'good' experiences. This is really asking what the 'pay off' is. How does this object, person, etc. make you feel good or likeable or competent . . .?

3 Produce your own passport. On one side of a piece of paper fill in the basic, 'flat' information about yourself. On the reverse side include more personal comments – about your likes and dislikes, your personality, the things that matter to you. What is the most important thing you want to say about yourself?

Rastafarians: Fire gonna fall next time

In these next three sections we shall look at people whose lives are dominated by a major idea. Something has become so special or important to them that it has become the basis of a complete *system* or *way of life*.

It's not difficult to spot a Rasta or Rastafarian. Maybe there are Rastas in your school or neighbourhood. Perhaps you're one yourself. They are a group of people with a strong commitment. What is it that binds them together?

1

▸The first great belief is that **God (Jah) has appeared as a man.** In the 1920s a Jamaican prophet, Marcus Garvey, predicted, 'Look to Africa when a black king shall be crowned.' In November 1930 the Prince Regent of Ethiopia, Ras Tafari, was crowned king and took the name Haile Selassie I. The true Rastafarian accepts and believes with his or her whole heart that Haile Selassie I is God. This is not just a cold belief. It's a crisis point — just as when you see something new and important for the first time. Rastafarians use phrases like, 'Ras Tafari passed over I,' 'Ras Tafari found I.' From that point of decision the whole world is changed. It looks different. You've become a new person.

2

▸The second great idea is **Africa. Africa is both a real place and a symbol.** Like the Jews in the Old Testament, the Rastafarians are a people on the move. Their great hope is to leave the countries where they are living at the moment and go back to their true homeland. Africa is the place from which all black people are descended. It's where the blacks have their roots. Africa is a country where the black man and woman can live freely, without being oppressed, with the dignity and self-respect that's due to all human beings.

▸**How important is it actually to get back to Africa?** This is not an easy question to answer. Some Rastafarians have physically returned and are living in Ethiopia at this moment. Many Rastafarians believe that the return to Africa will come only when Jah brings it about by a miracle. Meanwhile Rastafarians live and breathe Africa here in Britain. You have to 'live African' here – to be African in your heart. Living as a free, proud African now in London or Birmingham is just as important as actually getting on the boat and crossing the sea. But one belief is unshakeable: Africa is the final resting-place for all black people.

▸**In 1975 Emperor Haile Selassie I died.** You might think that this would cause problems for the movement. In fact this didn't happen. Some Rastafarians believe that the news of his death was a plot on the part of the Western, white world. He is not dead but in hiding. Others accept that he died but expect his resurrection. For some it's not important. Haile Selassie was a 'temporary embodiment' of Jah. The important thing about Haile Selassie is that Jah (God) appeared in the form of a *black man.*

▸**What's at the heart of these ideas?** Someone has said the Rastafarian movement has come out of *grief and suffering*. The history of the West Indians is one of slavery. Thousands of Africans were forcibly taken from their homes and shipped across to work plantations in the West Indies. They were treated in appalling ways and were handled as if they were non-persons, denied even the most basic human rights. Although slavery was abolished many years ago, the *memory* of the years of oppression remains, passed down from generation to generation. It's part of your people's history. It's easy to see how some West Indians in Britain might see this country as a white man's world. Rastas call it 'Babylon' – in the Bible that's the name for the old enemy of God's people. You can't expect anything good from 'Babylon' – teachers, employers, government, police will try to keep you down, turn you into a slave again. But one day 'the fire is gonna fall' and Babylon is going to collapse.

▶In the late seventies some of these ideas were expressed in what was then **a new kind of music – Reggae.** Bob Marley was the big name. His album, *Catch a fire,* said it all for hundreds of young blacks. 'Slave driver the table is turn / catch a fire so you gonna get burn.'

By 1977 Bob Marley was an international star. Many of his records seemed to be pushing revolution and defiance. 'Stand up for your rights, see the light' was telling Rastafarians to walk tall and let the world know that they couldn't be shoved around any more.

▶**Rastafarians show their commitment in visible ways.** First there's the *dreadlocks* – hair styled into masses of tight plaits. 'Locksing up' is a way of showing that Ras Tafari is alive. The *tams* or woolly hats, are also important because they reflect the red, green, gold and black of Ethiopia. Many Rastas carry *makutarias* or prayer sticks.

Rastafari even changes the way you speak. A Rastaman is an 'I-man'. Rastas will often say 'I and I'. In the Old Testament God refers to himself as 'I am'. So I can be one with God – an I-man. But that also means I can be one with you – not '*we*' or 'I and *you*' but 'I and I'. This is how people are bound together as brothers and sisters.

They also keep to a special diet, based on the Old Testament laws. They go for

'I-tal foods' (i.e. natural foods) – cereals, fruits and vegetables. Meat, fish and alcohol are banned. Canned foods are not I-tal. This creates problems for some Rastafarians who cannot always afford the more expensive I-tal foods. They sometimes have to eat like Babylon but hope and pray that Jah will forgive them.

Rastas will say that it's not all as clear-cut as this, of course. Not every West Indian who wears a tam and likes Reggae is a true Rasta. One Rastafarian said, 'Some blacks give us a bad name, beating up old ladies and that.' Sometimes white society is too quick to make snide remarks about Rastas, calling dreadlocks 'rats' tails' and prayer sticks 'pick axe handles' and assuming they're all out to smash the police. A Rastaman said, 'Rastas are about peace . . . race don't matter.' This is a bit of an exaggeration. The Rastafarian movement is certainly about being black and proud of it. It does look back on 400 years of white oppression. It looks forward to the collapse of 'Babylon' and a return to the promised land where blacks can be free.

Feminists: women are people too!

Sally is 17 and in the sixth form at Woodside Comprehensive. She's intelligent, pretty, petite and talkative. And just occasionally very annoyed.

Yes, well I suppose I would call myself a feminist, yes. I sort of got pushed into it once I started to notice certain things – just little things – but they all mount up.

'What sort of things?'

I'm not being unreasonable but I suddenly got tired of always being talked down to because I was a girl. Like being told I'm weak and emotional and likely to cry if things go wrong. To listen to men you'd think women were stupid.

My father actually said to me the other day, 'Don't worry your pretty little head about that. Leave it to your brother.' ?!!! I could've killed him. But my sister (she's 22) wired up their new cooker when she and her husband moved into their house. *She* wired it up. He was all for ringing the Electricity Board.

And another thing . . . Have you noticed how boys always insist on driving the car? I passed my driving test first time and so did my mum. But my two brothers – Britain's answer to Nelson Piquet – both *failed* first time. Yet you see these cars going round with 'Me' over the driving seat and 'Our lass' over the passenger seat. OK . . . some men are bigger, stronger, quicker than some women. So what? Most women can stand pain better. It's a well-known fact. There's no need for either sex to treat the other as inferior.

If you say all this in public, how do people react?

D'you mean aggro? Oh yes, plenty. Lads ask if you've burned your bra and when you're off to Greenham Common. And they call you a Lez. They get really threatened. But why should they? It's as if they can only feel safe if they're dominating. And there's always the arrogant ones who hold the Big Bang theory. Y'know'. . . 'all these women's libbers need is a good man and they'd straighten out.'

Is that hard to take?

ANSWER THI

It's not the boys I mind. It's the pressure from women that's difficult. You take my mum. She says I *ought* to clear away the dinner things and leave my brothers to watch telly. Now *why* is it my job specially? I'll take my turn but my mum just loves her chains.

Some feminists give you the idea they'd like to abolish men. What's your view on that?

Oh no, that's stupid. I like my boyfriend. I don't want him abolished. I want to be treated like a person, that's all. Some feminists are rude and aggressive. I know one girl who won't let boys open the door for her. They're just being polite. And there's supposed to be this feminist restaurant that doesn't allow men in and has got a notice up – 'No takeaways! Do not take our food away to feed men.' What good does that do? It just makes men annoyed. I don't want to abolish men or be rude to them (unless they ask for it) and I *don't* want to be a man. I'm proud I'm a girl but I also want to be treated like an individual and a person.

Don't you think you're exaggerating it all – just a bit?

You kidding? You want some examples? OK. How would you feel about these if you were female?

I have to walk past a garage to get to the shops. I'd like just once not to be a sex object. If I go at the tea-break the mechanics are all squatting on the pavement. It's murder walking past. 'Ooh, get 'em off, darling', 'What y'doing tonight?' and all that. If you do nothing you look snooty and if you say something you get a mouthful back.

I'd like not to be pigeon-holed. Don't assume that because I'm a girl I can't do science and won't want to do computing. Don't push me into Biology or Home Economics when I want to drive a tractor or be an engineer. Just imagine for a second that I might just . . . just not want to be a hairdresser or an air hostess. I might want to *fly* the plane, OK? Not be a glorified waitress.

But most girls don't drive tractors or turn out as engineers

I know that. I don't mind. But don't make it difficult for the ones who want to do something unusual. And don't make them feel peculiar or freaks. No double standards, OK? I'll give you an example. Why do we have just 'Mr' for men and 'Mrs' and 'Miss' for women? Why are men allowed to know that a woman is 'available' and women have to guess about the blokes? Why is it OK for Page 3 to show boobs every day but a full frontal male counts as obscene? Why is it if a boy plays around he's called 'a bit of a lad' – and it's all 'ho, ho, nudge, nudge' – if a girl does it, she's a 'slag' or a 'tart'?

And another thing. What about weddings? Your father 'gives you away'! Have you thought about that? 'Gives you away'! I don't mind if my Dad gives me away on my wedding day – 'cos I like him – but he doesn't *own* me. It is a bit insulting. (I'd also like to make a speech at the reception.)

It's all about power, isn't it? Men don't want to lose it.

What chance do you think you've got of turning back thousands of years of male dominance, then?

Things are changing. I'm not a way-out feminist, like a member of the Union, protesting and marching and all that. But I am a person who doesn't like being pushed around. I find I'm getting more ready to speak up for myself than I used to be. In discussions the boys often dominate – and the teachers encourage them. Well, that doesn't have to be . . .

Animal Liberation: who needs another shampoo?

The third example of commitment which we are going to look at is 'Animal Liberation.

"Surely there's enough suffering in the world to do with human beings without being bothered by animals. After all, they're obviously not as important as we are. Why bother?"

We're not saying all lives, animals, humans, insects and plants are equally valuable. We're not animal lovers. We're not sentimental about animals. The important questions are not:

Are animals like human beings?
Can animals think?
Can animals talk?
Can animals reason?

The important question is:
Can animals *feel pain?*

"Who says animals can feel pain?"

This might seem an impossible question to answer. Humans can't get into an animal's mind. But some experiments have given animals a *choice* to see what conditions they *prefer*. For example, chickens that had been kept in battery cages were given freedom to go back to the cages or run free in an outside run. They *chose* the outside run. Surprise, surprise.

And we can use our common sense: Is this animal happy? Is it feeling pain?

> Before beginning the test on my own I was instructed in how to apply the haemostats . . . The (monkey) was placed in the chair and the haemostat clamps were latched as tightly as possible onto his testicles. Terrified, he thrashed violently and screamed. This was repeated three times over a forty-five minute period so that I could witness a 'positive' reaction: an enraged creature, desperately thrashing against the restraints to escape the pain.

"Don't these reports exaggerate? Is it as bad as all that?"

It depends what you mean by bad.

▶ The USA began to train dolphins to carry limpet mines to fix on to enemy ships. Dolphins are intelligent and friendly. It's obscene to bring them into *our* wars.

▶ In Britain packs of dogs are trained to hunt down and kill foxes. Some people say the fox enjoys this.

▶ In 1982 the Home Office licensed over 4 million experiments on living animals, for testing drugs, pesticides, cosmetics and toiletries. Many experiments involved burning, scalding, exposure to irradiation, electric shock, interference with the brain, inserting painful substances into the eye.

> The Draize Test is the standard test applied to every substance, from cosmetics to oven cleaners, which might get into someone's eye . . . You start with six albino rabbits. You take each animal and check that the eyes are in good condition. Then, holding the animal firmly, you pull the lower lid away from one eyeball so that it forms a small cup. Into this cup you drop 100 milligrams of whatever it is you want to test. You hold the rabbit's eye closed for one second and then let it go. A day later you come back and see if the lids are swollen, the iris inflamed, the cornea ulcerated, the rabbit blinded in that eye.

“A lot of these experiments are necessary. You might discover a cure for cancer or prevent cosmetics damaging human beings or produce cheaper food.”

▶ A business man only cares about his profit. Why do we need 700 different kinds of shampoo? Just so that the cosmetics firms can make a bomb?

▶ We may have to take a slight drop in our standards of living. But in the West we eat too much anyway. And genuine free-range eggs taste better.

▶ In medical reserach many scientists say, ‘Let’s do this and see what happens.’ That doesn’t make it right to inflict pain on thousands of animals just in case you come up with a brilliant idea.

“What do animal liberators do?”

▶ The RSPCA gets convictions in the courts against people who mistreat animals.

▶ Some people wear badges like ‘Stop vivisection’; ‘Stop the seal culls’; ‘Save the whale’.

▶ Hunt saboteurs spread false trails to deceive the hounds.

▶ Often starting a publicity campaign against a particular firm is enough to make the firm take notice.

▶ The Animal Liberation Front is more militant. It attacks laboratories so that firms have to increase their security and pay higher insurance premiums. It has claimed to put rat poison into cans of food or cosmetics. The whole range has to be withdrawn from the shops just in case someone gets injured. This can cost a firm hundreds of thousands of pounds.

▶ The Animal Rights Militia is even more militant. It has used letter bombs and thrown red paint over women who wear real fur.

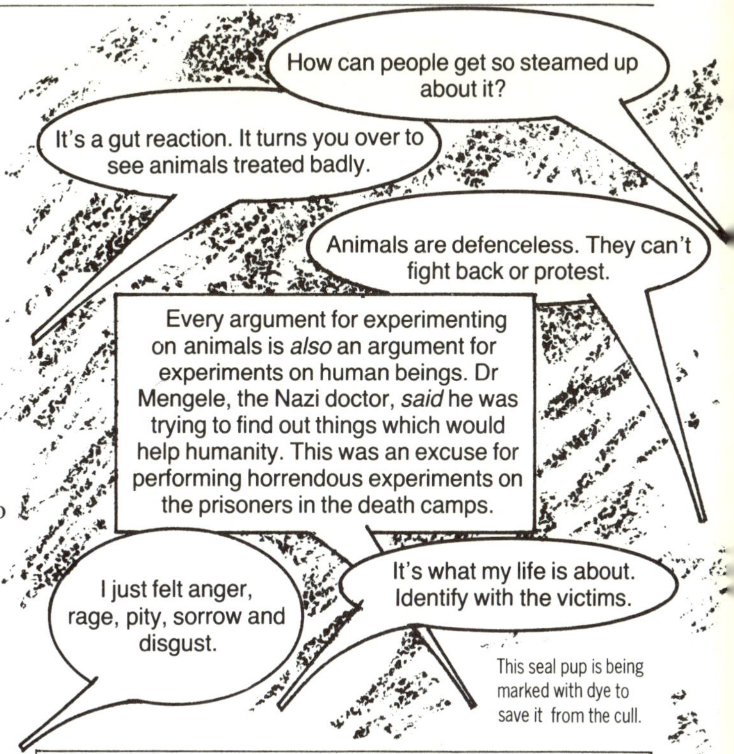

This seal pup is being marked with dye to save it from the cull.

FOLLOW UP ON COMMITMENTS

These questions are designed to help get inside the three commitments we've just been looking at.

1 Each 'cause' or 'commitment' is a complete system or way of life. Draw up a grid with three columns across the page and eight headings down the left hand margin. At the top of the columns put RASTAFARIANS, FEMINISTS, ANIMAL LIB. In the left hand margin put the following:

- Experience (i.e. what sort of experience pushed the person towards this commitment?)
- Evil (i.e. what evil or injustice are they fighting against?)
- Ideal World (i.e. what would their perfect world be like?)
- Motto (i.e. make up a short motto – not more than seven words – for each one)
- Objects (i.e. name two objects that might mean a lot to each one)
- People (i.e. Name two people who might be heros or heroines to them)
- Song (i.e. think of a song which sums up what they believe in)
- Pressure (i.e. give an example of some pressure that might make them keep quiet about their beliefs)

Some of the information you need is in the articles. For the rest you'll have to use your imagination and your ability to get inside their world.

2 Produce a poster on behalf of any of the three causes.

3 Argue about the rights and wrongs of any of the three commitments.

- Can you see evidence *for* the viewpoint: i.e. to suggest that they are right to take up the stand they have?
- Can you see evidence *against* the viewpoint: i.e. to suggest that they've got it wrong?

You might *debate* this in class or *discuss* it in a smaller group or *write* down your views individually.

CRUSADER QUIZ

Have you got what it takes to be a crusader?

Perhaps you already have a cause which gets you excited or angry. Even if you haven't at the moment, are you the sort of person who can take on the world without losing any sleep over it?

Check up on your crusading potential with this quiz.

1 A teacher declares that the whole class is going to be kept behind because two or three people were making a noise. This is thought to be very unfair. What do you do about it?
(a) Moan to your friends but turn up for the detention.
(b) Shop the three people who were the real cause of the trouble by means of an anonymous note to the staff room.
(c) Organize a deputation to see the teacher concerned in the lunch hour and ask if he will change his decision.

2 Think through all the tee-shirts you've got and all the badges you possess – the ones you wear, the ones in your room at home, the ones you've stuck on your guitar, your Maths book and the seat of your jeans.
How many are . . .
(a) rude?
(b) protesting about something?
(c) celebrating the delights of some product (food, alcohol, sweets) or some pop group?

3 You read in the local paper about some mothers who want a crossing patrol outside a primary school. They have organized a rota of mums to walk backwards and forwards across the road for the whole of the working day. The traffic jams caused by their action are enormous. What do you say?
(a) 'Stupid old biddies. If I were in a car 'd mow 'em down.'
b) 'Why don't you go and join them, Mum?'
c) 'That's typical of the Council, tight-sted, penny-pinching lot of misers.'

Score the following people and organizations on a three-point scale, here *** means you *strongly approve* of em; ** means 'So-so, they're OK'; * eans you *strongly disapprove* ('ought to banned'/ 'Doing it for the publicity', etc.)
Greenpeace
Bob Geldof
CND
Greenham Common women
Monster Raving Loony Party

5 It's Friday night. You have the choice of . . .
(a) playing records with a friend of the same sex.
(b) staying in and watching a thriller on the television.
(c) messing about down the Leisure Centre (not doing anything in particular but annoying the attendant)

6 Would the people in your class say that . . .
(a) you talked too much in discussions?
(b) you were a bit quiet?
(c) you didn't take part because you were always messing about?
(d) you said something if you felt you had something worth saying?

7 You've been given a 500-piece jigsaw for Christmas, Do you . . .
(a) start it but abandon it once *The Guns of Navarone* starts on the television?
(b) carry on working away until the thing is finished?
(c) invent a new game called 'Flicking bits of jigsaw at the dog'?

8 You're with your friends one evening and one of them starts to say malicious things about the love life of a girl/boy in your class. These tales are *very* insulting, *very* funny and (you happen to know) totally untrue. Do you . . .
(a) say, 'You're making all this up as you go along'?
(b) say nothing but laugh as loudly as anyone else?
(c) add a few juicy bits of your own?

9 A friend says, 'You're one of the most popular people in the class. Do you know why? It's because you never disagree with anyone. It's a real talent you've got for not stirring people up.'
Do you . . .
(a) say, 'Do you really think so?' and feel pleased at the compliment?
(b) feel slightly irritated but say nothing?
(c) say, 'You must be kidding! I'm always contradicting people'?

10 Have you ever got off your backside and protested about any injustices or campaigned for any cause at all? (Shouting 'That's not fair' at teachers doesn't count.) Briefly write down the details. (You can stop when you get to three examples.)

11 Who do you see yourself as . . .?
(a) St George?
(b) The Dragon?
(c) The damsel in distress?

ANSWERS THIS WAY

1. (a) 1; (b) 1; (c) 3.
2. (a) 2; (b) 3; (c) 1.
3. (a) 1; (b) 1; (c) 3.
4. Give yourself 1 mark for each three star rating and 1 mark for every one star rating. No marks for two star ratings. Maximum 5.
5. (a) 2; (b) 1; (c) 3.
6. (a) 3; (b) 1; (c) 1; (d) 3.
7. (a) 1; (b) 3; (c) 2.
8. (a) 3; (b) 1; (c) 2.
9. (a) 1; (b) 2; (c) 3.
10. Score 1 mark for every example up to three. Maximum 3.
11. (a) 3; (b) 3; (c) 1.

How did you rate?

27–35: Yes, you've got what it takes all right! In fact you've probably got the white horse saddled up already and are getting to work on the armour with the brillo pad. You're determined, with strong opinions and not afraid to voice them. You're impossible to live with but if you're about to ride off on another crusade any minute now, who cares? At least it will be quiet while you're away.

18–26: So-so. Inclined to sit on the fence a bit. And that's quite uncomfortable. You're easy going. You can get worked up if you want to but you really do enjoy the quiet life.

0–17: Oh dear! Muttering at the back of the crowd won't do. Get up the front and make a name for yourself. At the moment you're about as much use as a chocolate teapot.

What's special in religion?

We've been looking at things that people think are special, from teddy bears to life itself. So far there haven't been many religious examples. But, in fact, religion probably throws up more instances of special things than any other human activity.

The pictures on this page are all of special places. Stonehenge is a sacred place to those who follow the old religion. Hindus bathe in the sacred River Ganges. Muslims gather outside the mosque at Kano. And young Catholic Christians make the pilgrimage to Lourdes, seeking healing.

▸For example, you will find lots of **special objects**. The altar or table in Christian churches is not usually treated like any old piece of furniture. It's normally placed in a prominent position and often fenced off from the body of the church.

In Jewish homes a small box called a mezuzah is fastened to the doorpost. Jews touch it as they go in and out.

A Sikh values his turban. It is much more than a head-covering.

Statues of the Hindu gods and goddesses are treated with great respect, garlanded with flowers and offered food. They are not treated as 'just statues'. In the same way, in the Orthodox church, icons are never seen as 'just pictures'.

▸There are also **special places.** Jerusalem is a special city for Jews, Muslims and Christians. Mecca is the centre of the world for Islam. The Ganges is a special river for Hindus. And all over the world there are special places – shrines, churches, temples, even clearings in the forest or stone circles like Stonehenge.

▸There are **special people.** For Catholics the Pope is Christ's representative on earth. If a Muslim says the name of Muhammad he always says, 'Peace be upon him' immediately afterwards. Gurus and Holy Men are seen as people who are set apart in some way. Some Christians would view priests and nuns like this.

▸There is even **special language.** In some branches of Christianity Latin is used partly because it feels like an out-of-the-ordinary language. Hindus pronounce the syllable 'Om' to express a sense of mystery which is beyond words. In Judaism the name of God must not be written in full or pronounced. A West African church uses the word 'Ajjawworrakkabb' in its services. No one knows the meaning of this word. That's why it's special.

▸There are **special actions.** Muslims go through set positions of prayer and face Mecca while they do so. At one point they touch their forehead on the ground. Christians make the sign of the cross, or raise their hands in the

This may seem a complete ragbag.
▶Is it possible to make any sense out of these lists of special things?
▶Is there anything that will hold them all together?
▶Anything that will explain why some things have 'specialness' attached to them and others don't?

We need to discover the inside story.

air, or close their eyes when praying. Buddhists sit in the lotus position when meditating. These actions are all decided in advance. No one is making them up as they go along.

▶There is **special food.** Jews may eat chicken and duck but not lobster or pork. At a Hindu temple visitors will be given prasada. In their Holy Communion Christians eat bread and drink wine, but no one pretends that there's enough for a proper meal.

▶There are **special books.** Whether it's the Gita, the Guru Granth Sahib, the Bible, the Qur'an or the Torah, these books are all treated and used differently from the Telephone Directory or the *TV Times*.

FOLLOW UP

1 The best way of following up on this information would be to choose three or four of the examples mentioned and find out more about them. Concentrate on two questions:

▶what are the facts? (i.e. fill out the brief comment above with as much extra information as you can manage)
▶what are the meanings? (i.e. what do people believe about them? Why do they think they are special?)

For this exercise you will need to get some reference books from your teacher, or spend some time in the library.

Your answers will look more interesting if they can be presented visually in some way.

2 If your family is religious it might be possible for you to bring a special object to do with your religion and talk about it to the rest of the group.

The idea of the holy

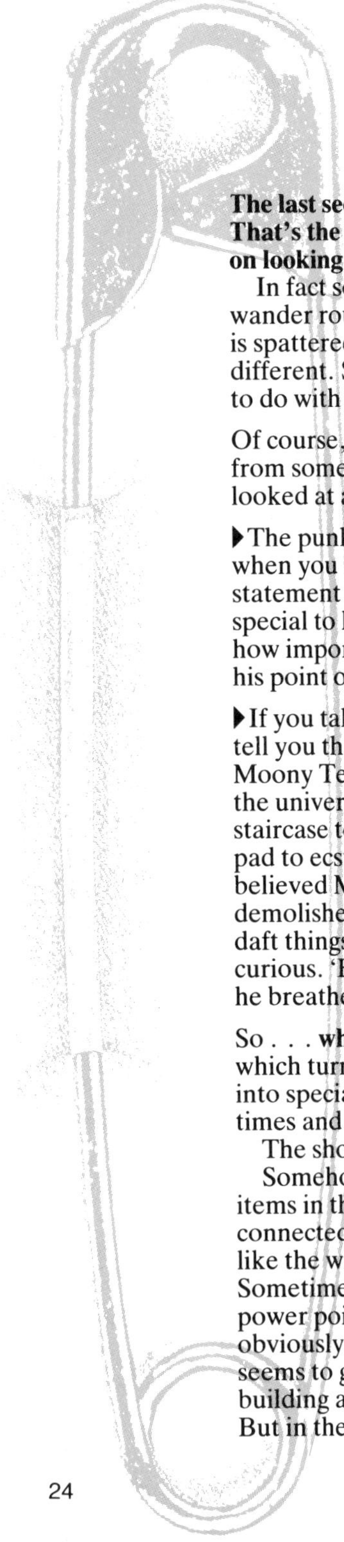

The last section looked like a rubbish-tip. Now we need to discover its inside story. That's the problem. Unless we can find the key that will unlock the door it will go on looking like junk.

In fact someone has said that religion is like a stained glass window. If you wander round the outside of the building you hardly notice it. It looks dirty and is spattered with bird droppings. But if you go inside . . . then everything looks different. Suddenly you see the most fantastic colours. From outside most things to do with religion look strange, puzzling or plain stupid.

Of course, religion isn't so different from some other special things we've looked at already.

▸The punk's safety pin 'makes sense' when you realize that it's part of a statement he wants to make. It's special to him and we can begin to see how important it is once we get inside his point of view.

▸If you talk to Arnold Grope he will tell you that stars shine over Number 9 Moony Terrace, that it is the centre of the universe, the bottom of the staircase to heaven, and the launching-pad to ecstasy. You have always believed Moony Terrace ought to be demolished. 'Why do you say all these daft things?' you ask, naturally curious. 'Because *SHE* lives there . . .' he breathes.

So . . . **what is the mystery ingredient** which turns the religious rubbish-tip into special or 'holy' objects, people, times and so on?

The short answer is 'God'.

Somehow, directly or distantly, the items in the last section are all connected up to the idea of God. It's like the wiring in your house. Sometimes the various bulbs and power points are wired up fairly obviously. Sometimes the wiring seems to go half-way round the building and branch off into loop lines. But in the end what makes the bulbs light up and the sockets live is the fact that they are all connected to the power source.

Unfortunately the word 'God' or 'Allah' or 'Krishna' or 'Yhwh' can be misleading and off-putting. Some people immediately think of Father Christmas, some of an old man in the sky, and others just find the term a total switch-off.

One expert preferred to talk about 'The *Holy*'. He said this was the *Big Word* in religion. What did he mean by it?

You can forget 'holes in the ground' and saints with haloes. When he said 'holy' he meant an experience that was full of mystery, power, fear and fascination. It terrifies you and attracts you at the same time. It is so awe-ful you want it to stop and so fantastic you wish it could go on for ever. You can't begin to describe it and yet people who have experienced it can't stop talking about it.

If you've had such an experience you don't need to be told about it. If you haven't then it's probably time for some examples. Don't worry for the moment if they don't seem to make much sense to you, or if they seem to be put in flowery language. Try to get the 'feel' of what's happening.

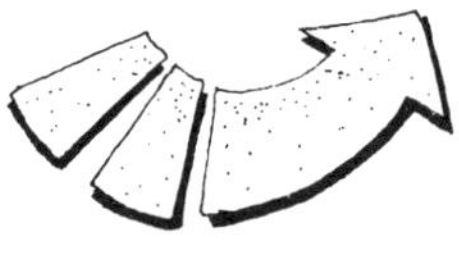

In the year that King Uzziah died I saw the Lord seated on a throne, high and exalted, and the train of his robe filled the temple. Above him were seraphs . . . And they were calling to one another:
'Holy, holy, holy is the Lord Almighty;
The whole earth is full of his glory.'
At the sound of their voices the doorposts and thresholds shook and the temple was filled with smoke.
'Woe to me!' I cried. 'I am ruined! . . . my eyes have seen the King, the Lord Almighty.'[1]

Trembling and bewildered, the women went out and fled from the tomb. They said nothing to anyone, because they were afraid.[2]

The Voice said three words in Arabic which were to shake the world: 'You are the messenger of God.' 'I was standing,' Muhammad is reported to have said, 'but I fell on my knees and dragged myself along while the upper part of my chest was trembling. I went in to Khadija and said, "Cover me, cover me!" until the terror had left me.[3]

There was a time when I stood there near the Ka'ba and I felt that I wasn't on earth at all. I was on a different plane completely separated from earth. It's an experience you get there that you can't explain, really, in words. You feel it, you experience it. It's really difficult, because the pilgrimage, the Hajj, is not easy on the physical body; but the experience you get is so different, so beautiful.[4]

For me, after I was filled with the Spirit, it was one of the happiest times of my Christian life, because I felt so much joy in myself, that I really – I got filled, one night in my bedroom, and when I went to bed I was so happy that I couldn't sleep. I was tossing and rolling, you know. I was really happy.[5]

It didn't matter that I didn't have control over my body. I didn't panic that I was sort of thinking I can't move my hand or I can't sit up. It was just a case of lying down and sort of feeling . . . engulfed. As if something was engulfing you to make you feel completely relaxed and sort of filled . . . And nothing really mattered . . . Just a state of restful ecstasy and it felt very light. It was dark in this hall thing we were in but it felt very sort of illuminated around me.

I thought they were all mad. But then, I don't know what happened, but I remember the feeling after one of the group meetings of coming back from the group over to where my tent was and – it was a weird feeling – it was just like God. I could feel God. He was sort of there and it was odd, and all of a sudden it was really real. It was just there. God was just there.

Something woke me up. There was something or somebody by my bed; I wasn't frightened. Within ten minutes the torment I'd felt, for some strange reason left me. I think I had more peace then than I'd had for a very long time . . . I have enough knowledge to know that there's somebody there, to know that I need never be so alone again.[6]

I saw the entire evening sky filled with meteorites which fell like snowflakes all around me. This again gave me this extraordinary feeling of vastness; the sense that the whole universe was one, that we were just a tiny speck in it; and yet I felt that my experience was important, in this vast sea of divinity.[7]

Each note vibrated in me, and when I finally was completely awake I realised it was a robin singing. It was still dark in the room. The sound seemed to move in me. Something in me responded with so much joy, I could not bear it. It became a pain, I felt as if I would burst. I jumped out of bed and ran through the house. I wanted to shout, to cry, to run, anything to relieve the pain of all that joy.[8]

* The Contents page tells you where each of these quotations comes from.

Fantastic!

This is a very odd title for a section. What we're going to try to do is to get inside the experience of the holy. This is bound to be difficult for anyone who has never had such an experience themselves. What other people say about it will sound like nonsense.

So let's start with some similar problems just to get at the size of the task.

▶Imagine you've got a headache. You mention this to your friend. She takes no notice, or says, 'Oh yeah . . . fascinating.' Apart from beating her over the head with a handy saucepan, how would you communicate what your headache feels like? Remember, it's not enough just to *say,* 'I've got a headache.' Somehow you've got to try to get over what your headache *feels* like. Think about the different ways you might use language . . . or pictures . . . or sounds . . . or actions . . . or your friend's past experience . . .

▶Imagine you are taken on a space ship to a planet where curved lines are totally unknown. Everywhere you look there are straight lines but no curves. Squares, rectangles, triangles, parallelograms – fine! But no curves, arcs, rugby balls or circles. You *know* there are shapes called circles. You have *seen* them when you were on earth. How do you try to communicate the idea of a circle to people who have never seen a curved line (and probably don't believe that circles exist)?

What kind of experience makes *you* go 'Wow!'? Is it doing a ton?

If you found these exercises difficult, you're beginning to get some idea of how difficult it is to communicate the *experience* of the *holy* to someone who's never had it.

The expert who wrote the book *The Idea of the Holy* actually thought it was impossible to describe the experience. That didn't stop him writing the book. He thought it might be possible for people to get a very rough idea of what he was talking about.

So let's start with some experiences you might have had . . .

▶Think of any experience you've had which made you go 'Wow! Yee-ha!

'Yowee! Kerflip!' or whatever it is you say when you run out of words. Is there an experience which you would describe as 'fantastic', 'out of sight', 'something else'?

Here are some examples of what other people have said in answer to that question:

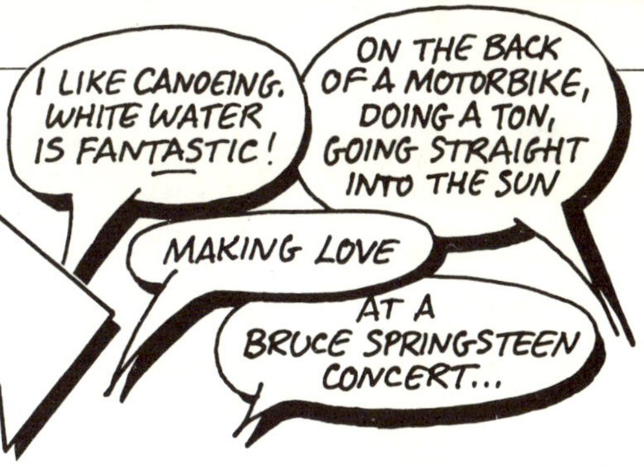

In one class a boy described how he'd fallen over while he was carrying a milk bottle. He'd gashed his hand really badly. He was *terrified* – because it was a serious injury and was going to need hospital treatment. But at the same time he was *fascinated* – because it was his blood (not someone else's) that was pumping over the pavement.

▶Try coming at the idea from another direction. What do you find mysterious . . . or 'spooky' or 'uncanny'? For example, one boy said it gave him a weird feeling to think about space.

“When you get to the end, there's always a bit more, isn't there? And then if you go to the end of that bit there's a bit more still. If I think about it for too long it gives me a headache.”

Another boy said,

“I remember this book I had as a kid. There was a picture of a man reading. And on the page he was looking at there was a picture of the same man reading the same book. And on the page of *that* book there was the same man . . . and so on. It was weird. It goes on and on for ever, don't it?”

▶Now try experiences of power. Have you ever been pole-axed by seeing something immensely powerful? So powerful that just thinking about it blew your mind? It might be a Russian shot putter or weight lifter. Or a vast cathedral. Or the speed of a jet fighter as it streaks across a quiet valley in Wales at the speed of sound.

“I remember taking my kids to see the cheetahs at the zoo. They're only very big cats, aren't they? We stood there watching them prowling round and round the cage, with all the muscles rippling. And I remembered that they can run at eighty miles an hour. And I suddenly got this vision of me doing seventy in the fast lane of the M1 and being overtaken by this thing screaming along the central reservation . . .”

▶What about meeting a hero, or a very famous person? One girl met the members of her favourite group after the concert. She said,

“I couldn't stop shaking. I couldn't get any words out. I just stood there like a lemon with my mouth open. I'd never seen them in the flesh before. Afterwards one of them shook hands with me. I didn't wash for a week.”

▶Sometimes people connect the holy with experiences of beauty or perfection. For example, when a baby is born the parents often say that it was the most beautiful experience of their lives and that the baby was so perfect it almost made them cry. 'Even her little finger nails are perfect.' But one man said he got the same feeling when he looked at a sheet of perfectly white paper, just before he was going to paint on it. Sometimes it's new snow, or absolutely still water, that does the trick.

These are all ways in which we can try to catch a glimpse of what people mean when they talk about experiencing the holy. It's a bit like describing the taste of new potatoes. Or explaining what red is to a blind person. But if you work away at these situations you might begin to make sense of the way religious people talk.

Religion: the unmentionable subject?

Religious-type experiences may seem strange to you. In fact you may not be able to make any sense of them at all. But, obviously, not everyone feels like this. For many years researchers in different countries have been trying to find out how many people have these experiences and what sort of people they are. Once you start to look into this question you get some surprising answers.

Notice that the surveys aren't looking just for 'churchy' feelings or just for people who go to places of worship. They're interested in experiences which can be called 'religious' even if you have to stretch the word beyond its usual meaning. Very often they ask questions something like these:

“Have you ever felt that your life has in any way been affected by some power beyond yourself?”

“Have you ever been aware of or influenced by a presence or power, whether you call it God or not, which is different from your everyday self?”

“Have you ever felt as though you were very close to a powerful spiritual force that seemed to lift you out of yourself?”

How would you reply to these invitations?

The actual replies are amazing. An astonishingly large number of people answer these questions with 'Yes'. Some go to a place of worship; some used to go but have now stopped; but many have never linked this kind of experience with churchgoing at all.

One researcher found that 62% of the people he contacted had had a 'religious' experience. Somebody has estimated that there are about 15 million people in Britain who come into this category.

When the results are analyzed a pattern begins to appear. These experiences often happen without warning, when someone is alone and in distress; they don't last for much longer than a few minutes; they are 'good' experiences; and they 'feel real', even 'more real than real life'.

One particular researcher, a man called David Hay, was surprised at the high numbers. He used to ask people, 'Have you ever told anyone about this?' Very often he got the answer, 'Oh, no, my friends would think I was weird.'

- An 18-year-old shop worker said, 'Never! Just laugh at me . . . well, they'd probably listen but they wouldn't understand.'
- Another man said, 'I'd tell the wife. I don't tell me mates. Otherwise they'd think I'd gone barmy.'

It looks as if our society puts pressure on people to keep quiet about their deep experiences if they are in the area of religion. In Victorian times sex was the unmentionable subject. Perhaps today it's religion. We have a hundred ways of making people feel slightly daft or embarrassing them.

For example, the media often show religious people as a bit soft; vicars are wimps and wallies; they talk in a sing-song voice and faint if they hear a swear word.

The high-cred leaders in our society are

- the hard man, like Rambo or the Exterminator
- the brainy scientist in a white coat
- the cool, sophisticated model, who

grabs her chance and has no time for sentimentality

- the sharp businessman who walks all over his competitors.

If the survey results are correct then about four or five people in every ten are walking about with the memory of an experience which has been absolutely fantastic and which they are too embarrassed to tell anybody about. That includes their best friends, who are probably walking about with the memory of an experience which has been absolutely fantastic and which they are too embarrassed . . . etc, etc, etc.

FOLLOW UP

1 Explore the idea of leaders in our society. Make a list of the big names in different areas of life. Who comes into your mind as the mega-stars in world politics, fashion, sport, films/videos, music – classical and pop – religion, TV?

More interesting than a list would be a quiz. Between you, collect about thirty photos of famous faces; the sort of people who you think might be recognized immediately without a caption. Stick them up on a large sheet of paper. Now see how many your group can identify. Count up the scores and produce a league table of famous people. How many of them are religious people?

2 Is it true that our society is hostile to religion? Do we live in a world where people are embarrassed to admit they've had religious experiences because others will think they are daft or soft?

What is the image of religion in your class? Try this word association game. Don't stop to think. Put down the first thought that comes into your head.

> When the word religion is mentioned
>
> WHAT WORD comes to mind first?
> WHAT OBJECT? WHAT PERSON?
> WHAT COLOUR? WHAT FEELING?
> WHAT BUILDING? WHAT ACTION?

Now evaluate the results. What's the general feeling? How good is the *image* of religion in your class?

Imagine you're working for an advertising firm with the task of 'improving the image of religion in our society'. Taking your time, think up the most positive list you can.

3 What topics in our society are people embarrassed to talk about or admit to feeling? Think about the different habits, or illnesses, or beliefs, or past record people have. Produce a list of OK and non-OK subjects. Can you explain why people feel this way?

What does it all add up to?

What we've been looking at is only one way of being religious, of course. There are other ways. And some religious people claim that they've never had a 'religious experience' like the ones we've been describing.

Just the same, the experience bit is important enough for us to concentrate on it. We've tried to make sense of the feelings people have when they think they encounter God or 'the holy'. And as we've seen right through this book, what you **feel**, what you **value**, and how you **act** are all connected.

How does this work for religion?

Here are people who have had an experience of the holy. It was a 'good' experience. In fact, it was *the* good experience to beat all others.

Because of this experience they **value** objects, people, places, books, times of the year. All these become little reminders of the great experience. They're not just reminders, either. They are ways of getting the experience all over again. You don't gaze at a photo of your girl-friend or boy-friend just to make sure you don't forget what they look like. The photo *does* remind you but it also produces all the right feelings – love, longing, desire and that gooey feeling in the pit of your stomach.

And because of all this they **organize their lives** round the one thing which is supremely valuable – more special than anything else.

This is why people often misunderstand religion. It's not really a hobby – like darts or bingo. Most religious people don't even feel that religion is something they decided to take up – like badminton or disco dancing. Something or someone 'grasped' them – got hold of them. In other words, they were reacting to something that got them first.

Books like this one are *not* trying to make anyone religious who isn't already. But they *are* trying to get you to look at religion, without prejudice, and understand the way it works. And often, looking at *someone else's* point of view helps you to see *your own* more clearly.

So that's where we'll end – where we started – with you.

For each of us, life revolves around the things we value most. It's the same for religious people: what they value most is their faith and experience of God – and they live accordingly.

What comes next is not a test. There aren't any right answers. When you've thought about what you want to put, you need to share it with a partner or with the group. Sharing means explaining, giving examples, comparing, asking questions and maybe, arguing.

● MAJOR MYSTERIES ●

Complete this sentence as many times as you want to.

'Something that has always puzzled me is . . .'

● BIG EXPERIENCES ●

Think of the biggest thing that's happened to you so far. For example, one 16-year-old boy picked the time when he was involved in a really bad car crash. A 15-year-old girl recalled the occasion when she went off to London with a 'Proovy' (a boy from the local Approved School), right against the orders of her parents.

What did you learn from that experience . . . about yourself . . . other people . . . what Life is like . . . Or anything else?

● STRONG OPINIONS ●

Complete this sentence as often as you want to until your anger runs out.

'Something that really makes me angry is when . . .'

● HERE I STAND ●

This part is slightly different. You'll find a lot of pairs below. You *have* to choose one of each pair. This is a *forced* choice. So you can't say 'I don't like either of them.'

If I have to choose I *prefer* . . .

- Honesty in everything/Nicking a bit never did any harm
- Something beautiful/Something useful
- Keeping/Sharing
- If you drop buttered toast it always falls butter side down/toast side down
- Death is the end/There's got to be something after death
- Taking risks/Playing safe
- Lots of people/Being on my own
- Strangers are interesting/Strangers are out to get you
- Forgiving/Keeping a grudge
- Sex is love/Sex is sex
- Doing/Thinking
- Things/People
- God/Coincidence
- Look after Number One/Think of others first
- Blowing my mind/Staying in control
- Getting/Giving
- Now/Wait
- Pleasure/Success
- Talking before fighting/Get them before they get you
- Money/Happiness

When you talk out your answers do you notice any differences between groups of people (e.g. the sexes)? What are the main differences between what you have chosen and what your parents would have chosen? Or what you would have put, say, five years ago?

What's it all add up to? It's time for the last page . . .

What you've produced is a rough map of the sort of person you are. The important thing is that it's your map, thought out and drawn by you, not by somebody else. The other point to remember is that it doesn't have to stay that way. Thinking, talking, growing, changing are some of the signs of life.